KU-535-295

The Scottish Collection

Scottish
QUOTATIONS

Hazel Mills

HarperCollins*Publishers*

Cover image:
The Chieftain by Joseph Simpson (United Distillers & Vintners)

HarperCollins Publishers
PO Box, Glasgow G4 0NB

First published 1999

Reprint 10 9 8 7 6 5 4 3 2 1 0

© HarperCollins Publishers, 1999

ISBN 0 00 472304 X

A catalogue record for this book is available from the British Library

All rights reserved

Printed and bound in Great Britain by The Bath Press

Contents

Scotland is indefinable; it has no unity except upon the map.

Robert Louis Stevenson (1850–94)

Scotland small? Our multiform, our infinite
   Scotland *small*?
Only as a patch of hillside may be a cliché corner
To a fool who cries 'Nothing but heather!'

Hugh MacDiarmid (1892–1978)

Then Scotland's right, and Scotland's might,
And Scotland's hills for me;
We'll drink a cup to Scotland yet
Wi' a' the honours three.

Henry Scott Riddell (1798–1870)

I Look on Switzerland as a sort of inferior Scotland.

Sidney Smith (1771–1845)

Scotland! thy weather's like a modish wife!
Thy winds and rains, forever arre at strife:
So Termagent, a while her Thunder tries,
And, when she can no longer scold – she cries.

Aaron Hill (1685–1750)

Scotland is bounded on the south by England, on the
   east by the rising sun. on the north by the Arory-
   bory-Alice, and on the west by Eternity

Nan (Anna) Shepherd (1983–1981)

The rose of all the world is not for me
I want for my part
Only the little white rose of Scotland
That smells sharp and sweet – and breaks the
heart.

Hugh MacDiarmid (1892–1978)

*S*eeing Scotland, Madam, is only seeing a worse England.
It is seeing the flower fade away to the naked stalk.

Samuel Johnson (1709–1784)

O Caledonia! stern and wild,
Meet nurse for a poetic child!
Land of brown heath and shaggy wood,
Land of the mountain and the flood,
Land of my sires! what mortal hand
Can e'er untie the filial band,
That knits me to thy rugged strand!

Sir Walter Scott (1771–1832)

*T*hat knuckle-end of England – that land of Calvin,
oat-cakes, and sulphur.

Sydney Smith (1771–1845)

*S*cotland is not a place, of course. It is a state of mind.
Probably every country is and we should be cautious
when we assume we are unique. Other people may be just
as crazy as we are.

Cliff Hanley (1922–)

Scotland is the country above all others that I have seen, in which a man of imagination may carve out his own pleasures. There are so many *inhabited* solitudes.

Dorothy Wordsworth (1771–1855)

This is my country,
The land that begat me.
These windy spaces
Are surely my own.
And those who here toil
In the sweat of their faces
Are flesh of my flesh
And bone of my bone.

Alexander Gray (1882–1968)

When shall I see Scotland again? Never shall I forget the happy days I passed there amidst odious smells, barbarous sounds, bad suppers, excellent hearts, and the most enlightened and cultivated understandings.

Sydney Smith (1771–1845)

Poor sister Scotland
Her doom is fell
She hasn't any more Stuarts to sell.

James Joyce (1882–1941)

Scotland is European, with its own sea-access to the springs of European thought.

Walter Elliot (1888–1958)

Scotland

There is nothing the Scots like better to hear than abuse of the English.

Pope Pius II (1405–1464)
[comment after a visit
to Scotland in 1435]

The Englishman assumes that nobody dislikes him while the Scotsman wouldn't be happy without an enemy.

Jimmy Hill

A desperate disease requires a dangerous remedy … one of my objects was to blow the Scots back again into Scotland.

Guy Fawkes (1570–1606)
[Explaining his proposed plot
to blow up Parliament]

When Hadrian built the Roman wall
To keep the horrid Scots away,
He didn't build it long enough
Or high enough or strong enough,
And look at us today!

J.B. Morton ('Beachcomber') (1893–1979)

Englishwoman: They're a sad race really. I blame the diet. I mean only two sorts of people eat porridge. Convicts … and Scotsmen.

Ian Pattison (1950–)

[Highland soldiers] are hardy, intrepid, accustomed to a rough country, and no great mischief if they fall.

General James Wolfe (1727–59)

I concede that the Scotch really do love learning. I gather, too, from unbiased sources that they starve their mothers and make gin-mules of their fathers to get it.

T. W. H. Crosland

*A*lack! They ever stream through ENGLAND's door
To batten on the Rich, and grind the Poor,
With furtive Eye and eager, clutching hand
They pass like *Locusts* through the Southern Land:
And line their purses with the yellow Gold,
Which for each Scotchman, London's pavements hold,
And in return, no matter where you find 'em
They brag of Scotland, now left safe behind 'em.

Anthony Powell (1905–)

*I*t requires a surgical operation to get a joke well into a Scotch understanding. Their only idea of wit … is laughing immoderately at stated intervals.

Sydney Smith (1771–1845)

*N*o McTavish
Was ever lavish.

Ogden Nash (1902–1971)

*I*t is never difficult to distinguish between a Scotsman with a grievance and a ray of sunshine.

P.G. Wodehouse (1881–1975)

*H*aving little else to cultivate, they cultivated the intellect. The export of brains came to be their chief item of commerce.

Stephen Leacock (1869–1944)

As Others See Us

*H*ere's tae us; wha's like us?
Gey few, and they're a' deid.
Scottish toast

*T*he People here are generally Civil, sagacious,
Circumspect, and Piously Inclined. Though Boethius
reports them to be great Drunkards ... Yet now it is not
soo: For though they use strong Ale and Beer (the nature
of the Climate requiring strong Liquor) yet generally they
are sober, and Temperate, but withal much given to
Hospitality and Feasting, very Civil and Liberal in their
Entertaining of Strangers.

Rev. James Wallace
[On the inhabitants of Orkney
in the seventeenth century]

*T*here are few more impressive sights in the world than a
Scotsman on the make.
J.M. Barrie (1860–1937)

*W*ith a stomach full of fish supper fat,
giro and Labour Party membership intact ...
Blackened but perfectly preserved at thirty-seven,
with the liver of a ninety-year-old.
William Hershaw (1957–)

*T*he typical Scot has bad teeth, a good chance of cancer, a
liver under severe stress and a heart attack pending. He
smokes like a chimney, drinks like a fish and regularly
makes an exhibition of himself.
Alan Bold (1943–)

*T*he Scots have always had a violence in their souls. Nowadays they express it at football; long ago religion was the outlet.

Robin Jenkins (1912–)

*G*uilt is of course not an emotion in the Celtic countries, it is simply a way of life – a kind of gleefully painful social anaesthetic.

A.L. Kennedy (1965–)

Rab C. Nesbitt: *W*e're some people us, by the way, the Scots! Wha's like us, eh? Not many, thank Christ.

Ian Pattison (1950–)

*W*e are for our own people. We want to see them happy, healthy and wise, drawing strength from cooperation with the peoples of other lands, but also contributing their full share to the general well-being. Not a broken-down pauper and mendicant, but a strong, living partner in the progressive advancement of civilization.

William Gallacher (1881–1965)
[The first Communist MP]

A Scot is a man who keeps the Sabbath, and everything else he can lay his hands on…

Chic Murray (1919–1985)

I think it possible that all Scots are illegitimate, Scotsmen being so mean and Scotswomen so generous.

Edwin Muir (1887–1959)

And Charlie he's my darling,
The young Chevalier.

Better lo'ed you'll never be,
And will you no come back again?
James Hogg (1770–1835)

The story of Wallace poured a Scottish prejudice in my
veins which will boil along there till the flood-gates of life
shut in eternal rest.

Robert Burns (1759–1796)

Busby emanated presence, substance, the quality of
strength without arrogance. No man in my experience
ever exemplified better the ability to treat you as an equal
while leaving you with the sure knowledge that you were
less than he was.

Hugh McIlvanney (1933–)
[on Sir Matt Busby, manager of
Manchester Unted]

En ma fin git mon commencement.
In my end is my beginning.
Mary, Queen of Scots (1542–1587)
[Motto embroidered with
her mother's emblem]

Here lies one who meant well, tried a little, failed
much: – surely that may be his epitaph, of which he need
not be ashamed.

Robert Louis Stevenson (1850–1894)

*H*ere lies he who neither feared nor flattered any flesh.

James Douglas, Earl of Morton (c. 1516–1581)
[Said during the burial of John Knox, 1572]

*B*eing Scotch, he didn't mind damnation and he gave the sun and the whole solar system only ninety million years more to live.

Stephen Leacock (1869–1944)
[on Lord Kelvin]

*T*he handsomest man ever to cut a throat.

Sir Winston Churchill (1874–1965)
[Describing Lord Lovat]

*H*e has his talents, his vast and cultivated mind, his vivid imagination, his independence of soul and his high-souled principles of honour. But then – ah, these buts! – St Preux never kicked the fire-irons, nor made puddings in his tea cup.

Jane Welsh Carlyle (1801–1866)
[Referring to Thomas Carlyle,
before their marriage]

*A*s long as actors are going into politics, I wish … that Sean Connery would become king of Scotland.

John Huston (1906–1987)

*T*here is something in Burns for every moment of a man's life, good days and bad.

H. V. Morton (1892–1979)

*A*n Englishman is never happy unless he is miserable;
a Scotsman is never at home but when he is abroad;
an Irishman is never at peace but when he's fighting.

Anonymous

*F*rom the lone shieling of the misty island
Mountains divide us, and the waste of seas –
Yet still the blood is strong, the heart is Highland,
And we in dreams behold the Hebrides
Fair these broad meads, these hoary woods are grand;
But we are exiles from our fathers' land.

John Galt (1779–1839)

*T*he sight of it gave me infinite pleasure, as it proved that
I was in a civilized society.

Mungo Park (1771–1806)
[Remark on finding a gibbet in an
unexplored part of Africa]

*B*reathes there the man, with soul so dead,
Who never to himself hath said,
This is my own, my native land!
Whose heart hath ne'er within him burned,
As home his footsteps he hath turned,
From wandering on a foreign strand!

Sir Walter Scott (1771–1832)

*I*t's hame and it's hame, hame fain wad I be,
O, hame, hame, hame to my ain countree!

Allan Cunningham (1784–1842)

They bore within their breasts the grief
That fame can never heal –
The deep, unutterable woe
Which none save exiles feel.

W.E. Aytoun (1813–1865)

Blows the wind today, and the sun and the
rain are flying,
Blows the wind on the moors today and now,
Where about the graves of the martyrs the
whaups are crying,
My heart remembers how! …

Be it granted to me to behold you again in
dying,
Hills of home! and to hear again the call;
Hear about the graves of the martyrs the pee-
wees crying,
And hear no more at all.

Robert Louis Stevenson (1850–1894)

There is no sunlight in the poetry of exile. There is only
mist, wind, rain, the cry of whaups and the slow clouds
abovedamp moorland. That is the real Scotland; that is the
Scotland whose memory wrings the withers of the far-
from-home; and, in some way that is mysterious, that is
the Scotland that even a stranger learns to love.

H. V. Morton (1892–1979)

A day oot o' Aiberdeen is a day oot o' life.
[Traditional Scottish saying]

*I*t was Glasgow – not Edinburgh – that was chosen as the 1990 European City of Culture. I'm sorry, Edinburgh, a castle above a shopping complex was simply not enough.

Arnold Brown

*A*uld Ayr, wham ne'er a town surpasses
For honest men and bonnie lasses.

Robert Burns (1759–1796)

Rab C. Nesbitt: *K*now the best thing yi can say about Rothesay? At least it isnae Dunoon. What a gaff that is, by the way. All the atmosphere of the interior of a wardrobe. Built for the nuclear age. Only toon in the hemisphere to have achieved total melt down of the human spirit. Even saying the name makes yi feel as if it's started drizzling on the roof of your mouth. Dun-oon!

Ian Pattison (1950–)

*B*eautiful city of Glasgow, I now conclude my muse,
And to write in praise of thee my pen does not refuse;
And, without fear of contradiction, I will venture to say
You are the second grandest city in Scotland at the
   present day.

William McGonagall (c. 1830–1902)

*E*nchanting … it shall make a delightful summer capital when we invade Britain.

Joseph Goebbels (1897–1945)
[on Edinburgh]

*S*t Andrews, that placid place of non-learning…

Alastair Reid (1926–)

*I*t is a large, stately, and well-built city, standing on a plain in a manner four-square, and the five principal streets are the fairest for breadth, and the finest built that I have ever seen in one city together.

Daniel Defoe (1660–1731)
[on Glasgow]

*A*iberdeen an' twal' mile roon,
Fife an' a' the lands aboot it,
Ta'en frae Scotland's runkled map
Little's left, an' wha will doot it?

David Rorie (1867–1946)

*S*tirling, like a huge brooch, clasps Highlands and Lowlands together.

Alexander Smith (1830–1867)

*P*ersons of good sense, I have since observed, seldm fall into disputation, except lawyers, university men, and men of all sorts that have been bred at Edinburgh.

Benjamin Franklin (1706–1790)

*C*umbernauld in a kilt – a description somewhat unfair on poor old Cumbernauld.

Tom Morton (1955–)
[on Inverness]

*H*istory will judge harshly the oppressive laws that have led to the virtual extinction of a unique culture from this beautiful place.

Inscription on the memorial cairn to the seven
men of Knoydart, commemorating
the land raid of 1848

*M*y heart's in the Highlands, my heart is not here,
My heart's in the Highlands a-chasing the deer,
A-chasing the wild deer and following the roe –
My heart's in the Highlands, wherever I go!

Robert Burns (1759–1796)

*W*e had one perfect day, blue and iridescent, with the bare northern hills sloping green and sad and velvety to the silky blue sea. There is still something of an Odyssey up there, in among the islands and the silent lochs: like the twilight morning of the world, the herons fishing undisturbed by the water, and the sea running far in, for miles, between the wet, trickling hills, where the cottages are low and almost invisible, built into the earth. It is still out of the world, and like the very beginning of Europe …

D.H. Lawrence (1885–1930)
[Of Skye]

*S*kye is often raining, but also fine: hardly embodied; semi-transparent; like living in a jelly fish lit up with green light.

Virginia Woolf (1882–1941)

*H*e who first met the Highlands' swelling blue
Will love each peak that shews a kindred hue,
Hail in each crag a friend's familiar face,
And clasp the mountain in his mind's embrace.

Lord Byron (1788–1824)

*G*lencoe is the only place in Scotland where they can't open a MacDonald's.

Bill Tidy

*I*n the highlands, in the country places,
Where the old plain men have rosy faces,
And the young fair maidens
Quiet eyes.

Robert Louis Stevenson (1850–1894)

*A*s a girl Caroline Macdonald had suffered from the Lone Shieling complex.

Compton MacKenzie (1883–1972)

*I*t isn't Skye, but it really is a lovely place, only spoiled by the people. Far too many of them.

Annie S. Swan (1859–1953)
[Of Oban]

*W*hen we turned the corner to go into the renowned Fingal's Cave, the effect was splendid, like a great entrance into a vaulted hall … The sea is immensely deep in the cave. The rocks under water, were all colours – pink, blue, and green – which had a most beautiful and varied effect.

Queen Victoria (1819–1901)

Highlands & Islands

Whether scaling Etive
Of the shifting faces,
Or on the summit of Blaven,
Sheet-ice glistening
Through walls of mist,
It is all one. The tracks
We pursue are ours;
The zone we would enter
Not the mountains, but ourselves.

Stewart Conn (1936–)

What better than a Wilderness, to liberate the mind.

Stewart Conn (1936–)
[On John Muir, naturalist]

Here the crow starves, here the patient stag
Breeds for the rifle. Between the soft moor
And the soft sky, scarcely room
To leap or soar.

T.S. Eliot (1888–1965)
['Rannoch Moor']

Nothing endured at all, nothing but the land ... The land was forever, it moved and changed below you, but was forever.

Lewis Grassic Gibbon (1901–1935)

September leaves drip crystal from the bush plum. Under each freighted branch a blush of sleek fruit, pendant gold and violet.

Walter Perrie

*W*hat would the world be, once bereft
Of wet and of wildness? Let them be left,
O let them be left, wildness and wet;
Long live the weeds and the wilderness yet.
              Gerard Manley Hopkins (1844–1889)
                              ['Inversnaid']

A mist of memory broods and floats,
The border waters flow;
The air is full of ballad notes
Borne out of long ago.
                      Andrew Lang (1844–1912)
                    [The river Tweed at twilight]

*H*eather is harsh to tears
and the rough moors
give the buried face no peace
but make me rise,
and oh, the sweet scent, and purple skies!
                  Kathleen Raine (1908–)

    *S*tars lay like yellow pollen
    That from a flower has fallen;
    And single stars I saw
    Crossing themselves in awe;
    Some stars in sudden fear
    Fell like a falling tear.
                  Andrew John Young (1885–1971)

*T*he bank was green, the brook was full of breamis,
The stanneris clear as stern in frosty nicht.
                      William Dunbar (c. 1460–c. 1525)

For so long as but a hundred of us remain alive, we will in no way yield ourselves to the dominion of the English. For it is not for glory, nor riches, nor honour that we fight, but for Freedom only, which no good man lays down but with his life.

Declaration of Arbroath, 1320

The bird, the beast, the fish eke in the sea,
They live in freedom everich in his kind;
And I a man, and lackith liberty.

James I of Scotland (1394–1437)

The rank is but the guinea's stamp,
The man's the gowd for a' that …

For a' that, an' a' that,
It's comin yet for a' that,
That man to man the world o'er
Shall brithers be for a' that.

Robert Burns (1759–1796)

Equality is the soul of liberty; there is, in fact, no liberty without it.

Frances Wright (1795–1852)

*R*och the wind in the clear day's dawin,
Blaws the cloods heelster-gowdie ow'r the bay,
But there's mair nor a roch wind blawin
Through the great glen o the warld the day.

Hamish Henderson (1919–)
['The Freedom Come-All-Ye']

*T*he sense of the equality of all men which is a feature
that has distinguished Scottish from English society has its
roots in the Presbyterian culture with its emphasis on
Bible study and its denial of priesthood …

Allan Massie (1938–)

*L*iberty was ever the tradition of my fathers, and, among
us, no person avails, but rather reason.

Saint Columbanus

A! fredome is a noble thing!
Fredome mayss man to haiff liking;
Fredome all solace to man giffio:
He levys at ess that frely levys!

John Barbour (c. 1316–1395)

England is not all the world.

Mary, Queen of Scots (1542–1587)
[Said at her trial, 1586]

This is an end of an auld sang.

Earl of Seafield
[On signing the Act of Union, 1707]

Minds like ours, my dear James, must always be above national prejudices, and in all companies it gives me true pleasure to declare, that, as a people, the English are very little indeed inferior to the Scotch.

Christopher North (1785–1854)

We have become the caterpillars of the island, instead of its pillars.

Sir Walter Scott (1771–1832)
[Comment on the Union]

See how the double nation lies;
Like a rich coat with skirts of frieze:
As if a man in making posies
Should bundle thistles up with roses.
Whoever yet a union saw
Of kingdoms, without faith or law.

Jonathan Swift (1667–1745)

Norway, too, has noble wild prospects; and Lapland is remarkable for prodigious noble wild prospects. But, Sir, let me tell you, the noblest prospect which a Scotchman ever sees, is the high road that leads him to England!

Samuel Johnson (1709–1784)

$\mathcal{A}$ Scots mist will weet an Englishman to the skin.
[Traditional saying]

$\mathcal{B}$lack be the day that e'er to England's ground
Scotland was eikit by the Union's bond.
Robert Fergusson (1750–1774)

$\mathcal{T}$hirty millions, mostly fools.
Thomas Carlyle (1795–1881)
[When asked what the population
of England was]

$\mathcal{L}$ook at the food – oatcakes, haggis, broth – it's all
peasant fare. This was a peasant country before the
Union.
Sir Nicholas Fairbairn (1933–1995)

$\mathcal{I}$ understand that perfectly. We feel very much the same
in Scotland.
Queen Elizabeth the Queen Mother (1900–)
[To a Boer who told her he could not bring himself to
forgive the British for having conquered his country]

$\mathcal{G}$od help England if she had no Scots to think for her!
George Bernard Shaw (1856–1950)

$\mathcal{S}$cotland's greatest days have ben since the Union. Our
greatest economic growth, our cultural flowering, our art
and our heritage come from the last three hundred years.
Ian Lang (1940–)

England & The Union

*T*rue Patriotism is of no Party.

Tobias Smollett (1721–1771)

*T*he enemies of Scottish nationalism are not the English, for they were ever a great and generous folk, quick to respond when justice calls. Our real enemies are among us, born without imagination.

R.B. Cunninghame Graham (1852–1936)

*T*he difference between devolution and evolution is that devolution takes longer.

Ewen Bain (1925–1989)

*S*top the world, Scotland wants to get on.

Winnie Ewing (1929–)

*H*aving a national identity is a bit like having an old insurance policy. You know you've got one somewhere but often you're not entirely sure where it is. And, if you're honest, you have to admit you're not too clear what the small print means.

William McIlvanney (1936–)

*N*obody ever celebrated Devolution Day.

Alex Salmond (1955–)

*A*s far as I am concerned, Scotland will be reborn when the last minister is strangled with the last copy of the *Sunday Post*.

Tom Nairn (1932–)

Nemo me impune lacessit.
Wha daur meddle wi' me.
Motto of the Scots Crown

*I*t cam' wi' a lass, and it'll gang wi' a lass.
James V (1512–1542)
[On the rule of the Stuart dynasty in Scotland]

I will govern according to the common weal, but not according to the common will.
James VI of Scotland and I of England (1566–1625)

I will end with a rule that may serve for a statesman, a courtier, or a lover – never make a defence or apology before you be accused.
Charles I (1600–1649)

*W*ho will not sing *God save the King*
Shall hang as high's the steeple;
But while we sing *God save the King*,
We'll ne'er forget the People!
Robert Burns (1759–1796)

A king is an insult to every other man in the land.
Andrew Carnegie (1835–1919)

*T*he monarch is a person and a symbol. He makes power and state both intelligible and mysterious.
Sir Ian Gilmour (1926–)

*T*here is no art which one government sooner learns of another than that of draining money from the pockets of the people.

Adam Smith (1723–1790)

A deep-seated Radicalism is the chief element of the Scottish political tradition.

Hugh MacDiarmid (1892–1978)

*U*ncle Harry was an early feminist ... Our family would often recount how, at a race-meeting in Ayr, he threw himself under a suffragette.

Arnold Brown

*H*e is used to dealing with estate workers. I cannot see how anyone can say he is out of touch.

Lady Caroline Douglas-Home (1937–)
[Referring to her father's suitability
for his new role as prime minister]

*A*s I took my seat it was said by political pundits that 'a chill ran along the Labour back benches looking for a spine to run up'.

Winnie Ewing (1929–)
[On entering Westminster after winning
a 1967 by-election for the SNP]

*A*nti-English passion…gives the nationalist movement a poisoned strength that can only lead to racism and chauvenism; at best, a burning hatred for Jimmy Hill is a poor substitute for a positive vision of Scotland reborn as a modern, inventive and enlightened social democracy in Europe.

Joyce McMillan (1952–)

*H*ow many Scottish Office civil servants does it take to change a light bulb?
None. Twelve of them write a report 'The New Darkness Explained: A Guide for Businessmen'.

Anonymous

*T*here is a story that when Mrs Thatcher first met Gorbachev he gave her a ball-point and she offered him Labour-voting Scotland.

Nicholas Shakespeare (1957–)

*H*appy the man who belongs to no party,
But sits in his ain house, and looks at Benarty.

Sir Michael Malcolm of Lochor

*H*e had all the virtues of a Scottish Presbyterian, but none of the vices.

Menzies Campbell (1941–)
[Of John Smith, leader of the Labour Party]

29

Some have meat and cannot eat,
Some cannot eat that want it:
But we have meat and we can eat,
Sae let the Lord be thankit.

Robert Burns (1759–1796)
['The Selkirk Grace']

One whisky is all right; two is too much; three is too few.

Highland saying

One often yearns
For the land of Burns.
The only snag is
The haggis.

Lils Emslie

There are only two rules for drinking whisky. First, never take whisky without water, and second, never take water without whisky.

Chic Murray (1919–1985)

Bannocks and a share of cheese
Will make a breakfast that a laird might please.

Allan Ramsay (1686–1758)

There are two things a Highlander likes naked, and one of them is malt whisky.

F. Marian McNeill (1885–1973)

A sense of proportion is anathema to the Glasgow drinker. When he goes at the bevvy it is a fight to the death

Hugh McIlvanney (1933–)

*F*irm and erect the Caledonian stood,
Old was his mutton, and his claret good;
Let him drink port, an English statesman cried –
He drank the poison and his spirit died.

John Home (1722–1808)
[On the high duty on French wine, claret being
'the only wine drunk by gentlemen in Scotland']

I think I have made it clear how important drink is to the
Scottish character. Is it any wonder how many
Glaswegians hold teetotallers in such great contempt? In
Glasgow, we've always enjoyed the ancient ceremony of
throwing teetotallers into pubs on Saturday nights.

Arnold Brown
[From an evening class introducing
local customs to Jewish immigrants]

*G*o sad or sweet or riotous with beer
Past the old women gossiping by the hour,
They'll fix on you from every close and pier
An acid look to make your veins run sour.

George MacKay Brown (1921–1996)

*G*et yer haggis right here! Chopped heart and lungs,
boiled in a wee sheep's stomach! Tastes as good as it
sounds!

Groundskeeper Willie (*The Simpsons*)

*A*t funerals, four rounds of whisky were considered due
to wounded affection and departed worth, and respect
was shown to the dead by the intoxication of the living.

Rev. Charles Rogers

Food & Drink

*Y*ou are hereby ordered to fall upon the Rebells, the McDonalds of Glenco, and putt all to the sword under seventy, you are to have a speciall care that the old fox and his sones doe upon no account escape your hands.

Order for the massacre of Glencoe, 1692

*F*hairshon swore a feud
Against the clan M'Tavish;
Marched into their land
To murder and to rafish;
For he did resolve
To extirpate the vipers,
With four-and-twenty men
And five-and-thirty pipers.

W.E. Aytoun (1813–1865)

*H*istory can show few benign mergings of people with people. Flame and blood is always the cement.

George MacKay Brown (1921–1996)

*S*till from the sire the son shall hear
Of the stern strife, and carnage drear,
Of Flodden's fatal field,
Where shiver'd was fair Scotland's spear,
And broken was her shield!

Sir Walter Scott (1771–1832)

*N*o great man lives in vain. The History of the world is but the Biography of great men.

Thomas Carlyle (1795–1881)

*T*he Scots have a strong and pervasive sense of history, yet all too often they prefer the romantic myth to the complicated truth.

Tam Dalyell (1932–)

*W*hat foreign arms could never quell
By civil rage and rancour fell.
Tobias Smollett (1721–1771)

*T*he whole gaudy, part-faded, part-patched-up tapestry of battles, midnight plots, child-kings, beleaguered queens, scheming earls and brimstone preachers that was held up before us as our country's history … had us enthralled.

D.R. Sutherland

*H*istory does not repeat itself. Historians repeat each other.

A.J. Balfour (1848–1930)

*H*appy the people whose annals are blank in history-books!

Thomas Carlyle (1795–1881)

*L*adies and gentlemen. This is your guard speaking. We are now in Scotland. Please observe two minutes' silence for the Battle of Flodden, the Highland Clearances and Scotland's non-appearance in the 1994 World Cup.

Arnold Brown
[As the train crosses the
border from England]

*W*e think them verray naturall fules,
That lernis ouir mekle at the sculis.
Sir David Lindsay (c. 1490–1555)

*E*ducation makes a people easy to lead, but difficult to
drive; easy to govern, but impossible to enslave.
Lord Henry Brougham (1778–1868)

*M*uch had he read,
Much more had seen; he studied from the life,
And in th' original perus'd mankind.
Dr John Armstrong (1709–1779)
['The Schoolmaster']

*T*o live for a time close to great minds is the best kind of
education.
John Buchan (1875–1940)

*E*xperience teaches
that it doesn't.
Norman MacCaig (1910–1996)

A university which does not have a philosophy section
has lost the right to be known as a university.
James Kelman (1946–)

*T*o me education is a leading out of what is already there
in the pupil's soul. To Miss Mackay it is a putting in of
something that is not there, and that is not what I call
education, I call it intrusion.

Muriel Spark (1918–)

*Y*ou were educated at Fettes and sent down from Edinburgh University. What could be more English that that?

Alan Melville (1910–)

*G*ie me ae spark o' Nature's fire,
That's a' the learning I desire.
Robert Burns (1759–1796)

*E*very school needs a debating society far more than it needs a computer. For a free society, it is essential.

Malcolm Rifkind

*T*he schoolmaster is abroad, and I trust more to him, armed with his primer, than I do to the soldier in full military array, for upholding and extending the liberties of his country.

Lord Henry Brougham (1778–1868)

*T*he true University of these days is a Collection of Books.

Thomas Carlyle (1795–1881)

*T*he most devilish thing is 8 times 8 and 7 times 7 it is what nature itselfe cant endure.

Marjory Fleming (1803–1811)

*A*ll men who have turned out worth anything have had the chief hand in their own education.

Sir Walter Scott (1771–1832)

I knew a very wise man who believed that … if a man were permitted to make all the ballads, he need not care who should make the laws of a nation.

Andrew Fletcher of Saltoun (1655–1716)

A coo and a cauf
Cut in hauf.

William Hershaw (1957–)
[On Damien Hirst's entry for the
Turner Prize for contemporary art]

*H*appiness dies, love fails, but art is forever.

Margaret Oliphant (1828–1897)

*T*here is but one art – to omit! O if I knew how to omit, I would ask no other knowledge. A man who knew how to omit would make an *Iliad* of a daily paper.

Robert Louis Stevenson (1850–1894)

*S*ome of my plays peter out and some pan out.

J.M. Barrie (1860–1937)

*A*rt is for everyone – paint, like a piece of music, is the most international thing I know.

Richard Demarco (1930–)

The Arts

When I hear the words 'Arts Council' I reach for my water pistol.

Ian Hamilton Finlay (1925–)

Art is the flower – Life is the green leaf. Let every artist strive to make ... something that will convince the world that there may be – there are things more precious – more beautiful, more lasting than life.

Charles Rennie Mackintosh (1868–1928)

Public art is art that the public can't avoid.

George Wyllie (1921–)

The professional art world is becoming a conspiracy against the public.

Julian Spalding (1947–)

The best artist is not the man who fixes his eye on posterity, but the one who loves the practice of his art.

Robert Louis Stevenson (1850–1894)

Modernism is the acceptance of the concrete landscape and the destruction of the human soul.

Eduardo Paolozzi (1924–)

I never had the least thought or inclination of turning Poet till I once got heartily in love, and then rhyme and song were, in a manner, the spontaneous language of my head.

Robert Burns (1759–1796)

*T*he Scots are incapable of considering their literary geniuses purely as writers or artists. They must be either an excuse for a glass or a text for the next sermon.

George Malcolm Thomson

*B*ooks are good enough in their own way, but they are a mighty bloodless substitute for life.

Robert Louis Stevenson (1850–1894)

A book is a friend whose face is constantly changing.

Andrew Lang (1844–1912)

> *A* Scottish poet maun assume
> The burden o' his people's doom,
> And dee to brak' their livin' tomb.
>
> Mony ha'e tried, but a' ha'e failed.
> Their sacrifice has nocht availed.
> Upon the thistle they're impaled.

Hugh MacDiarmid (1892–1978)

*O*ur principal writers have nearly all been fortunate in escaping regular education.

Hugh MacDiarmid (1892–1978)

*J*oin a Highland regiment, me boy. The kilt is an unrivalled garment for fornication and diarrhoea.

John Masters (1914–)

*B*efore the Union [the kilt] was considered by nine Scotchmen out of ten as the dress of a thief.

Lord MacAulay (1800–1859)

*I*n 1782 the decrees prohibiting tartan and the wearing of the kilt were rescinded, and in 1822 when George IV came to Edinburgh ... the old Highland dress became suddenly fashionable, and tailors ever since have been busily inventing new tartans.

Eric Linklater (1899–1974)

Here's to it!
The fighting sheen of it,
The yellow, the green of it,
The white, the blue of it,
The swing, the hue of it,
The dark, the red of it,
Every thread of it!

The fair have sighed for it,
The brave have died for it,
Foemen sought for it,
Heroes fought for it,
Honour the name of it,
Drink to the fame of it –
THE TARTAN!

Murdoch Maclean

National Dress

'There's nae place like hame,' quoth the de'il, when he found himself in the Court of Session.

Proverb

Hang a thief when he's young and he'll no steal when he's auld

Lord Braxfield (1722–1799)

Let them bring me prisoners, and I'll find them law.

Lord Braxfield (1722–1799)

Laws were made to be broken.

Christopher North (1785–1854)

Not proven. I hate that Caledonian *medium quid*. One who is not *proven guilty* is innocent in the eye of law.

Sir Walter Scott (1771–1832)

A lawyer without history or literature is a mechanic; a mere working mason; if he possesses some knowledge of these, he may venture to call himself an architect.

Sir Walter Scott (1771–1832)

Who thinks the Law has anything to do with Justice? It's what we have because we can't have Justice.

William McIlvanney (1936–)

*W*e who deal in words must strive to keep language pure and wholesome; and it is hard work, as hard almost as digging a stony field with a blunt spade.

George MacKay Brown (1921–1996)

*S*ince we began to affect speaking a foreign language, which the English dialect is to us, humour, it must be confessed, is less apparent in conversation.

Alexander Carlyle (1722–1805)

*B*e not the slave of Words.

Thomas Carlyle (1795–1881)

*A*ll speech, written or spoken, is a dead language, until it finds a willing and prepared hearer.

Robert Louis Stevenson (1850–1894)

*T*he curse of Scottish literature is the lack of a whole language, which finally means the lack of a whole mind.

Edwin Muir (1887–959)

I have heard them sing,
like a heart broken child deserted by its father …

And the rising words are unknown to me, but all
is half known, like a childhood story dimly remembered.

I have heard them sing
and so now I can believe that if there ever was an Eden
they must have spoken Gaelic there.

William Hershaw (1957–)
['On Hearing the Psalms Sung in Gaelic']

*T*he Highlander who loses his language loses his world.

Iain Crichton Smith (1928–1998)

*O*ch, I wish you hadn't come right now;
You've put me off my balance.

I was just translating my last wee poem
Into the dear auld Lallans.

Alan Jackson (1938–)

MAKARS' SOCIETY
GRAN' MEETIN'
THE NICHT
TAE DECIDE THE
SPELLIN'
O' THIS POSTER

Tom Leonard (1944–)

*I*n Glasgow, the majority of people don't communicate in
English, but in some sort of dialect.

Lorenzo Amuroso
[Italian footballer playing for
Glasgow Rangers]

*T*here are probably more households in Scotland where Urdu is spoken than there are Gaelic-speaking ones.

Allan Massie (1938–)

*H*ow exhilarating it was to sojourn once more in Glasgow, that charming citadel of tradition and culture. By a happy chance my arrival coincided with the ancient and picturesque Festival of Hogmanay or, as it is known in the native patois, RA BIG BOOZE-UP.

It was my good fortune to meet with a gentleman who invited me to accompany him to the sacred Hogmaniacal rites at a residence in the remote Southern terrain of the city called RASOOSIDE.

When I suggested that it might be expedient to engage a taxicab my companion mentioned a lady's name. 'NORAH!' he said, 'NORAHBLIDDICHANCE.' Before I could question him as to the lady's identity he made certain obscure references to snow and the Yukon … 'SNOWFAUR,' he stated, 'YUKONHOOFIT'.

Stanley Baxter and Alex Mitchell

*B*e merry, man! and tak nocht far in mind
The wavering of this wrechit world of sorrow;
To God be hummle, and to the friend be kind,
And with thy neebouris glaidly len' and borrow.

William Dunbar (c. 1460–c. 1525)

*W*isdom denotes the pursuing of the best ends by the best means.

Francis Hutcheson (1694–1746)

*W*hatever mitigates the woes or increases the happiness of others, this is my criterion of goodness; and whatever injures society at large, or any individual in it, this is my measure of iniquity.

Robert Burns (1759–1796)

I consider the world as made for me, not me for the world: it is my maxim therefore to enjoy it while I can, and let futurity shift for itself.

Tobias Smollett (1721–1771)

*W*hen an idea is dead it is embalmed in a textbook.

Patrick Geddes (1854–1932)

*T*hat action is best, which procures the greatest happiness for the greatest numbers.

Francis Hutcheson (1694–1746)

*K*nowledge, which is the bugbear of tyranny, is to liberty, the sustaining staff of life.

Frances Wright (1795–1852)

*O*f what use is philosophy ... if it cannot teach us to do or suffer?

Sir Walter Scott (1771–1832)

*T*o be honest, to be kind – to earn a little and to spend a little less, to make upon the whole a family happier for his presence, to renounce when that shall be necessary and not be embittered, to keep a few friends, but these without capitulation – above all, on the same grim condition, to keep friends with himself – here is a task for all that a man has of fortitude and delicacy.

Robert Louis Stevenson (1850–1894)

I don't believe in principles. Principles are only excuses for what we want to think or what we want to do.

Sir Compton Mackenzie (1883–1972)

*E*ve and the apple was the first great step in experimental science.

James Bridie (1888–1951)

*T*he scientific acquisition of knowledge is almost as tedious as a routine acquisition of wealth.

Eric Linklater (1899–1974)

*B*e happy while y'er leevin,
For y'er a lang time deid.
Scottish motto

*T*he life of every man is a diary in which he means to write one story, and writes another; and his humblest hour is when he compares the volume as it is with what he vowed to make it.
J.M. Barrie (1860–1937)

*T*he best-laid schemes o' mice an' men
Gang aft agley,
An' lea'e us nought but grief an' pain,
For promis'd joy!
Robert Burns (1759–1796)

*C*ustom, then, is the great guide of human life.
David Hume (1711–1776)

*C*hoose life. Choose mortgage payments; choose washing machines; choose cars; choose sitting oan a couch watching mind-numbing and spirit-crushing game shows, stuffing junk food intae yir mooth. Choose rotting away …
Irvine Welsh (1957–)

*L*ife's for living… I had never been told it when young, and … I haven't fully learnt it yet; but at least I now realise how much I've missed, and how many mistakes I've made.
Lord Reith (1889–1971)

Rab C. Nesbitt: Helluva life awthegither in't it? I mean if the present disnae get yi, the past jumps up and whaps yi on the napper. I'd four brothers all snuffed it. I survived coz I was the only one that could understand the claim form for Family Credit.

Ian Pattison (1950–)

Give to me the life I love,
Let the lave go by me,
Give the jolly heaven above
And the byway nigh me.
Bed in the bush with stars to see,
Bread I dip in the river –
There's the life for a man like me,
There's the life for ever.

Robert Louis Stevenson (1850–1894)

O grant me, Heaven, a middle state,
Neither too humble nor too great;
More than enough, for nature's ends,
With something left to treat my friends.

David Mallet (c. 1705–1765)

Our business in this world is not to succeed, but to continue to fail, in good spirits.

Robert Louis Stevenson (1850–1894)

What is life but a veil of affliction?

Tobias Smollett (1721–1771)

The Heart of Man, we are told, is deceitful and desperately wicked. However that may be, it consists of four chambers, the right ventricle, the left ventricle, the left auricle, the right auricle...

James Bridie (1888–1951)

Man's Unhappiness, as I construe, comes of his Greatness; it is because there is an Infinite in him, which with all his cunning he cannot quite bury under the Finite.

Thomas Carlyle (1795–1881)

Man's inhumanity to man
Makes countless thousands mourn!

Robert Burns (1759–1796)

Man is a creature who lives not upon bread alone, but principally by catchwords.

Robert Louis Stevenson (1850–1894)

Ever since the First World War there has been an inclination to denigrate the heroic aspect of man.

Sir Compton Mackenzie (1883–1972)

$\mathcal{N}$ature, who makes the perfect rose and bird,
Has never made the full and perfect man.

Alexander Smith (1830–1867)

On earth there is nothing great but man; in man there is
nothing great but mind.

Sir William Hamilton (1788–1856)

Then gently scan your brother man,
Still gentler sister woman;
Tho' they may gang a kennin wrang,
To step aside is human.

Robert Burns (1759–1796)

$\mathcal{W}$e never remark any passion or principle in others, of
which, in some degree or other, we may not find a
parallel in ourselves.

David Hume (1711–1776)

$\mathcal{M}$en are never so good or so bad as their opinions.

Sir James Mackintosh (1765–1832)

*F*or God's sake give me the young man who has brains enough to make a fool of himself!

Robert Louis Stevenson (1850–1894)

I am not young enough to know everything.

J.M. Barrie (1860–1937)

*Y*outh is the time to go flashing from one end of the world to the other both in mind and body; to try the manners of different nations; to hear the chimes at midnight; to see sunrise in town and country; to be converted at a revival; to circumnavigate the metaphysics, write halting verses, run a mile to see a fire, and wait all day long in the theatre to applaud Hernani.

Robert Louis Stevenson (1850–1894)

*O*ne's prime is elusive. You little girls, when you grow up, must be on the alert to recognise your prime at whatever time of your life it may occur. You must then live it to the full.

Muriel Spark (1918–)
[The Prime of Miss Jean Brodie]

I've told so many lies about my age I've made my children illegitimate.

Jessie Kesson (1916–1994)

Rab C. Nesbitt: *I* hate middle age. Too young for the bowling green, too old for Ecstasy.

Ian Pattison (1950–)

*O*ur hearts are young 'neath wrinkled rind:
Life's more amusing than we thought.

Andrew Lang (1844–1912)
[On middle age]

*W*ith expectation beating high,
Myself I now desired to spy;
And straight I in a glass surveyed
An antique lady, much decayed.

Elizabeth Hamilton (1758–1816)

*B*eing over seventy is like being engaged in a war. All our friends are going or gone and we survive amongst the dead and the dying as on a battlefield.

Muriel Spark (1918–)

*A*fter a certain distance, every step we take in life we find the ice growing thinner below our feet, and all around us and behind us we see our contemporaries going through. By the time a man gets well into the seventies, his continued existence is a mere miracle.

Robert Louis Stevenson (1850–1894)

*U*nto the deid gois all Estatis,
Princis, prelatis, and potestatis,
Baith rich and poor of all degree:
Timor Mortis conturbat me.

William Dunbar (c. 1460–c. 1525)

*T*o die will be an awfully big adventure.

J.M. Barrie (1860–1937)

*R*emember man, as thou goes by,
As thou art now so once was I,
As I am now so must thou be,
Remember man that thou must die.

Headstone in Straiton, Ayrshire

I am dying as fast as my enemies, if I have any, could
wish, and as cheerfully as my best friends could desire.

David Hume (1711–1776)

*H*ere in the body pent,
Absent from Him I roam,
Yet nightly pitch my moving tent
A day's march nearer home.

James Montgomery (1771–1854)

*G*rieve not that I die young. Is it not well
To pass away ere life hath lost its brightness?

Lady Flora Hastings (1806–1839)

*W*hile other people's deaths are deeply sad, one's own is
surely a bit of a joke.

James Cameron (1911–1985)

*D*eath, when it approaches, ought not to take one by
surprise. It should be part of the full expectancy of life.
Muriel Spark (1918–)

A silent conquering army,
The island dead,
Column on column, each with a stone banner
Raised over his head.
George Mackay Brown (1921–1996)

*T*o live in hearts we leave behind
Is not to die
Thomas Campbell (1777–1844)

*B*eautiful Railway Bridge of the Silv'ry Tay!
Alas, I am very sorry to say
That ninety lives have been taken away
On the last Sabbath day of 1879,
Which will be remember'd for a very long time.
William McGonagall (c. 1830–1902)

*H*ere lies interr'd a man o' micht
They ca'd him Malcolm Downie
He lost his life ae market nicht
By fa'ing aff his pownie
Aged 37 years
Gravestone Inscription

A dead woman bites not.
Patrick, Sixth Lord Gray (d. 1612)
[Advocating the execution of
Mary, Queen of Scots]

Death

53

So far I fallen was in loves dance,
That suddenly my wit, my countenance,
My heart, my will, my nature, and my mind
Was changit right clean in another kind.
James I (1394–1437)

All love is lost but upon God alone.
William Dunbar (c. 1460–c. 1525)

Strange is the love you have for your children. It creeps
into your life furtively like a stray cat unsure of its wel-
come, and then suddenly it has occupied every cell of
your being.
Ewan MacColl (1915–1989)

It is by loving, and not by being loved, that one can come
nearest the soul of another.
George MacDonald (1824–1905)

Lord Rosebery sat by his fireside,
Beside his bonny leddy:
'Shall we dae the thing ye ken,
Or shall we hae our dinner?'
'As my lord pleases,' said she then –
'But dinner isnae ready.'
Anonymous

It is better to break one's heart than to do nothing with it.
Margaret Kennedy

Ae fond kiss, and then we sever!
Ae fareweel, and then forever! ...

Had we never lov'd sae kindly,
Had we never lov'd sae blindly,
Never met – or never parted –
We had ne'er been broken-hearted.

Robert Burns (1759–1796)

It is very rarely that a man loves
And when he does it is nearly always fatal.

Hugh MacDiarmid (1892–1978)

O, love, love, love!
Love is like a dizziness;
It winna let a poor body
Gang about his biziness!

James Hogg (1770–1835)

So long as we love we serve; so long as we are loved by
others, I would almost say that we are indispensable; and
no man is useless while he has a friend.

Robert Louis Stevenson (1850–1894)

True love's the gift which God has given
To man alone beneath the heaven:
It is the secret sympathy,
The silver link, the silken tie,
Which heart to heart, and mind to mind,
In body and in soul can bind.

Sir Walter Scott (1771–1832)

*A*a are guid lasses, but whaur do the ill wives come frae?
Traditional saying

*A*h! gentle dames, it gars me greet,
To think how monie counsels sweet,
How monie lengthen'd, sage advices
The husband frae the wife despises!
Robert Burns (1759–1796)

*E*very man who is high up loves to think that he has done
it all himself; and the wife smiles, and lets it go at that.
It's our only joke. Every woman knows that.
J.M. Barrie (1860–1937)

*I*t was very good of God to let Carlyle and Mrs Carlyle
marry one another and so make only two people
miserable instead of four.
Samuel Butler (1835–1902)

*R*omances paint at full length people's wooings,
But only give a bust of marriages:
For no one cares for matrimonial cooings.
There's nothing wrong in a connubial kiss:
Think you, if Laura had been Petrarch's wife,
He would have written sonnets all his life?
Lord Byron (1788–1824)

*T*here was altogether too much candour in married life;
it was an indelicate modern idea, and frequently led to
upsets in a household, if not divorce.
Muriel Spark (1918–   )

*M*arriage is a wonderful invention. But then again, so is a bicycle repair kit.

Billy Connolly (1942–)

*T*he awe and dread with which the untutored savage contemplates his mother-in-law are amongst the most familiar facts of anthropology.

Sir James Frazer (1854–1941)

*H*e's a Scotsman. He got married in the backyard so the chickens could get the rice.

Bob Hope (1903–)

*T*he road to success is filled with women pushing their husbands along.

Lord Dewar (1864–1930)

A woman who takes her husband about with her every-where is like a cat that goes on playing with a mouse long after she's killed it.

Hector Hugh Munro (Saki) (1870–1916)

*T*o marry is to domesticate the Recording Angel. Once you are married, there is nothing left for you, not even suicide, but to be good.

Robert Louis Stevenson (1850–1894)

*T*he beds of married love are islands in a sea of desire

Edwin Morgan (1920–)

We can't for a certainty tell
What mirth may molest us on Monday;
But, at least, to begin the week well,
Let us all be unhappy on Sunday.

Charles, Lord Neaves (1800–1876)

Can a Man be a Christian on a Pound a Week?

Keir Hardie (1856–1915)
[Title of pamphlet, 1901]

Yet I am here, a chosen sample,
To show Thy grace is great and ample:
I'm here a pillar o' Thy temple,
Strong as a rock,
A guide, a buckler, and example
To a' Thy flock!

Robert Burns (1759–1796)

An atheist is a man who has no invisible means of support.

John Buchan (1875–1940)

What the Reformation did was to snuff out what must otherwise have developed into the most brilliant national culture in history.

Fionn MacColla (1906–1975)

If Jesus Christ were to come to-day, people would not even crucify him. They would ask him to dinner, and hear what he had to say, and make fun of it.

Thomas Carlyle (1795–1881)

Lutherans are like Scottish people, only with less frivolity.

Garrison Keillor (1942–)

I think Calvinism has done more damage to Scotland than drugs ever did.

R.D. Laing (1927–1989)

Ane wad maist trow some people chose
To change their faces wi' their clo'es,
And fain was gar ilk neibour think
They thirst for goodness as for drink.

Robert Fergusson (1750–1774)
[On Sundays]

I hope I will be religious again but as for reganing my charecter I despare for it.

Marjory Fleming (1803–1811)

One's religion is whatever he is most interested in, and yours is Success.

Sir J.M. Barrie (1860–1937)

No one can be an unbeliever nowadays. The Christian apologists have left one nothing to disbelieve.

Hector Hugh Munro (Saki) (1870–1916)

Done is a battell on the dragon blak;
Our campioun Christ counfoundit hes his force;
The yettis of hell ar brokin with a crak,
The signe triumphall rasit is of the croce.

William Dunbar (c. 1460–c. 1525)

*N*ae man can sair two maisters: aither he will ill-will the tane an luve the tither, or he will grip til the tane an lichtlifie the tither. Ye canna sair God an Gowd baith.

The Bible (The New Testament in Scots)

*A*dversity is sometimes hard upon a man; but for one man who can stand prosperity, there are a hundred that will stand adversity.

Thomas Carlyle (1795–1881)

*W*hat vails your kingdome, and your rent,
And all your great treasure;
Without ye haif ane mirrie lyfe,
And cast aside all sturt, and stryfe.

Sir David Lindsay (c. 1490–1555)

*W*hat is fame? an empty bubble;
Gold? a transient, shining trouble.

James Grainger (c. 1721–1766)

O, gie me the lass that has acres o' charms!
O, gie me the lass wi' the weel-stockit farms!

Robert Burns (1759---1796)

*S*urplus wealth is a sacred trust which its possessor is bound to administer in his lifetime for the good of the community.

Andrew Carnegie (1835–1919)

'No one has ever said it,' observed Lady Caroline, 'but how painfully true it is that the poor have us always with them!'

Hector Hugh Munro (Saki) (1870–1916)

Gif thou has micht, be gentle and free;
And gif thou stands in povertie,
Of thine awn will to it consent;
And riches sall return to thee:
He has eneuch that is content.

William Dunbar (c. 1460–c. 1525)

Cash payment is not the sole nexus of man with man.

Thomas Carlyle (1795–1881)

Everyone lives by selling something.

Robert Louis Stevenson (1850–1894)

I'm living so far beyond my income that we might almost be said to be living apart.

Hector Hugh Munro (Saki) (1870–1916)

Poverty keeps together more homes than it breaks up.

Hector Hugh Munro (Saki) (1870–1916)

It was said that he gave money away as silently as a waiter falling down a flight of stairs with a tray of glasses.

Billy Connolly (1942–)
[Of Andrew Carnegie]

The secret of my success over the 400 metres is that I run the first 200 metres as hard as I can. Then, for the second 200 metres, with God's help, I run faster.

Eric Liddell (1902–1945)

They'll be dancing in the streets of Raith tonight.
BBC radio broadcast from London in 1963, after Raith Rovers (from Kirkcaldy) defeated Aberdeen in a Scottish Cup tie

Football has taken the place of religion in Scotland.

Robin Jenkins (1912–)

Football confers nationality on the Scots because, as some academics have argued, [Scotland] is a stateless nation.

Arnold Kemp

Brilliant. Tell him he's Pelé.

John Lambie, football manager
[On hearing that Partick Thistle striker Colin McGlashan could not remember who he was after suffering a head injury]

Until a generation ago, kids would happily play football in the streets until it was too dark to see the ball. Now they can stage matches on the home computer and if they did go out for a kick-about in the street, there is a good chance they would be run over by a juggernaut.

Andy Roxburgh (1943–)

Some people think football is a matter of life and death. I don't like that attitude. I can assure them it is much more serious than that.

Bill Shankly (1914–1981)

I love fishing. It's like transcendental meditation with a punchline.

Billy Connolly (1942–)

We do have the greatest fans in the world but I've never seen a fan score a goal.

Jock Stein (1922–1985)
[Remark during the World Cup in Spain, 1982]

The Scots have won something more valuable than the trophy itself – a place in the hearts of other nations as the contest's true sportsmen.

The Times leader article, June 1998
[After the opening match of the World Cup 1998, in which Scotland lost to Brazil]

Golf is a thoroughly national game. It is as Scotch as haggis, cockie-leekie, high cheek-bones, or rowanberry jam.

Andrew Lang (1844–1912)

The critic who decries walking the Munros because it means climbing dozens of boring hills is commenting not on the richness of the hills but on his own dulled vision.

Hamish Brown (1934–)

COLLINS

Other titles in *The Scottish Collection* series include:

ISBN 0 00 472326 0

ISBN 0 00 472259 0

ISBN 0 00 472325 2

Classic Malts   *Scottish Verse*   *Scottish Recipes*
Homelands of the Clans